MY FIRST BOOK OF FREN

MY FIRST BOOK OF

FRENCH
VOCABULARY

INVADER

INTRODUCTION

Welcome to your first French vocabulary book. The words are arranged in sections with lively illustrations to help you to learn French. Remember that in French, **le** before a word means it is masculine; **la** is feminine. If the word begins with a vowel, **l'** is used; (m) after the word indicates that it is masculine and (f) that it is feminine.

Explanation of symbols

sing. The French word is in the singular.

plural The French word is in the plural.

sent-ence The French word is used in a short sentence to show its meaning.

vocab. New French words which have a connection with the main word.

CONTENTS

sing. **la mère**
mother

plural les mères
mothers

sentence Ma **mère** est très gentille.
My mother is very nice.

vocab.

la famille	*family*
la femme	*woman*
la grand-mère	*grandmother*
l'épouse (f)	*wife*

sing. **le père**
father

plural les pères
fathers

sent-ence Mon **père** est médecin.
My father is a doctor.

vocab.

les parents	*parents*
l'homme (m)	*man*
le grand-père	*grandfather*
l'époux (m)	*husband*

sing.

la sœur
sister

plural

les sœurs
sisters

sent-ence

Ma **sœur** aime rire.
My sister likes to laugh.

vocab.

la fille	*daughter*
le bébé	*baby*
grand	*big*
petit	*small/little*

sing. **le frère**
brother

plural les frères
brothers

sent-ence Mon **frère** est malade.
My brother is ill.

vocab.

le fils	*son*
le petit enfant	*toddler*
l'enfant (m/f)	*child*
l'adulte (m/f)	*adult*

sing. **le cousin**
cousin (male)

plural les cousins
cousins (m/f)

sent-ence Mon **cousin** siffle.
My cousin is whistling.

vocab.

l'oncle (m)	*uncle*
la tante	*aunt*
la cousine	*cousin (f)*
rendre visite à, visiter	*to visit*

sing. **la nièce**
niece

plural les nièces
nieces

sent-ence J'aime jouer avec ma **nièce**.
I like playing with my niece.

vocab.

jouer	*to play*
rire	*to laugh*
pleurer	*to cry*
crier	*to shout*

sing. **l'aspirateur** (m)
vacuum-cleaner

plural les aspirateurs
vacuum-cleaners

sent-ence L'**aspirateur** fait du bruit.
The vacuum-cleaner is noisy.

vocab.

le ménage	*housework*
le tapis	*carpet*
la poussière	*dust*
nettoyer	*to clean*

sing.

le seau
bucket

plural

les seaux
buckets

sent-ence

Le **seau** est rouge.
The bucket is red.

vocab.

plein	*full*
vide	*empty*
l'eau (f)	*water*
remplir	*to fill*

15

sing. **l'éponge** (f)
sponge

plural les éponges
sponges

sent-ence Je ne trouve pas mon **éponge**.
I can't find my sponge.

vocab.

sale	*dirty*
propre	*clean/neat*
la fenêtre	*window*
laver	*to wash*

sing. **l'échelle** (f)
ladder

plural les échelles
ladders

sent-ence Pierre grimpe à l'**échelle**.
Peter climbs up the ladder.

vocab.

le plafond	*ceiling*
au-dessus	*above*
au-dessous	*beneath*
grimper	*to climb*

○ LE MENAGE

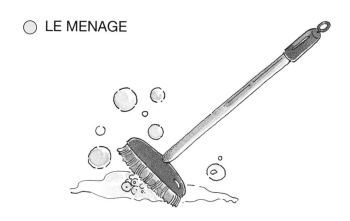

sing. **le balai**
broom

plural les balais
brooms

sentence Je cherche le **balai**.
I am looking for the broom.

vocab.

la pelle à poussière	*dustpan*
le sol	*floor*
balayer	*to sweep*
la poubelle	*dustbin*

18

sing.

le savon
soap

plural

les savons
cakes of soap

sent-ence

Je me lave avec du **savon**.
I wash myself with soap.

vocab.

le porte-savon	*soap dish*
le lavabo	*washbasin*
le miroir	*mirror*
se laver	*to wash oneself*

sing. **la marmite**
saucepan

plural les marmites
saucepans

sent-ence La **marmite** est sur la cuisinière.
The saucepan is on the cooker.

vocab.

cuisiner	*to cook*
la cuisine	*kitchen*
la cuisinière	*cooker*
remuer	*to stir*

sing. **la poêle**
frying-pan

plural les poêles
frying-pans

sentence La viande est dans la **poêle**.
The meat is in the frying-pan.

vocab.

le cuisinier	*the cook*
l'huile (f)	*oil*
la crêpe	*pancake*
frire	*to fry*

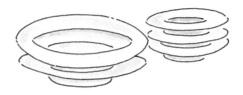

sing. **l'assiette** (f)
plate

plural les assiettes
plates

sent-ence Mon **assiette** est vide.
My plate is empty.

vocab.

la soucoupe	*saucer*
la tasse	*cup*
le verre	*glass*
boire	*to drink*

○ LE MENAGE

sing. **le couvert**
cutlery

plural les couverts
sets of cutlery

sent-ence Le **couvert** est dans ce tiroir.
The cutlery is in this drawer.

vocab.

la fourchette	*fork*
le couteau	*knife*
la cuiller	*spoon*
la table	*table*

23

● LA CLASSE

sing. **l'institutrice** (f)/**l'instituteur** (m)
teacher

plural les institutrices/instituteurs
teachers

sent-ence L'**institutrice** écrit au tableau.
The teacher writes on the blackboard.

vocab.

l'école (f)	*school*
le tableau	*blackboard*
la craie	*chalk*
écrire	*to write*

24

sing.	**la fille** *girl*
plural	les filles *girls*
sent-ence	La **fille** va à l'école. *The girl is going to school.*

vocab.	la classe	classroom
	la leçon	lesson
	l'élève (m/f)	pupil
	étudier	to study

sing. **le garçon**
boy

plural les garçons
boys

sent-ence Le **garçon** a un devoir.
The boy has some homework.

vocab.

le devoir	*homework*
le français	*French*
l'anglais (m)	*English*
le calcul	*mathematics*

26

sing. **l'ami** (m)
(boy) friend

plural les amis (m/f)
friends

sentence Je joue avec mon **ami**.
I play with my friend.

vocab.

l'amie (f)	*(girl) friend*
gentil, amical	*friendly*
sourire	*to smile*
aimer	*to like/love*

27

sing. **le cahier**
exercise book

plural les cahiers
exercise books

sent-ence J'écris dans mon **cahier**.
I write in my exercise book.

vocab.

le mot	*word*
la phrase	*sentence*
l'erreur (f)	*mistake*
l'exercice (m)	*exercise*

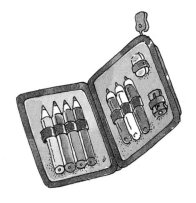

sing.

le plumier
pencil case

plural

les plumiers
pencil cases

sent-ence

J'ai un nouveau **plumier**.
I have a new pencil case.

vocab.

le crayon	*pencil*
la gomme	*rubber*
le taille-crayon	*pencil sharpener*
le cartable	*schoolbag*

sing. **le livre**
book

plural les livres
books

sent-ence Nous lisons un **livre**.
We are reading a book.

vocab.

le titre	*title*
la page	*page*
le dictionnaire	*dictionary*
lire	*to read*

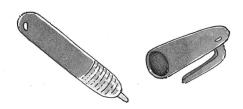

sing. **le stylo à bille**
ballpoint pen

plural les stylos à bille
ballpoint pens

sentence Le **stylo à bille** n'écrit pas.
The ballpoint pen will not write.

vocab.

l'encre (f)	*ink*
la tache	*blot*
le dessin	*drawing*
la lettre	*letter*

sing.

la règle
ruler

plural

les règles
rulers

sent-ence

Il trace une ligne avec une **règle**.
He draws a line with a ruler.

vocab.

la ligne	*line*
le chiffre	*figure*
dessiner, tracer	*to draw*
mesurer	*to measure*

sing. **la chanson**
song

plural les chansons
songs

sent-ence Nous chantons une **chanson**.
We are singing a song.

vocab.

la musique	*music*
la note	*note*
chanter	*to sing*
siffler	*to whistle*

sing.

le melon
melon

plural

les melons
melons

sent-ence

Je compte un **melon**.
I count one melon.

vocab.

un/une	*one*
vert	*green*
le pépin	*pip*
la queue	*stalk*

sing. **le kiwi**
kiwi fruit

plural les kiwis
kiwi fruits

sent-ence Je mange deux **kiwis**.
I eat two kiwi fruits.

vocab.

deux	*two*
le jus	*juice*
doux	*sweet*
aigre	*sour*

(sing.) **la pomme**
apple

(plural) les pommes
apples

(sent-ence) J'achète trois **pommes**.
I buy three apples.

(vocab.)

trois	*three*
le pommier	*apple tree*
le jus de pomme	*apple juice*
acheter	*to buy*

sing.
la pomme de terre
potato

plural
les pommes de terre
potatoes

sent-
ence
J'épluche quatre **pommes de terre**.
I peel four potatoes.

vocab.

quatre	*four*
la pelure	*peel*
la purée	*mashed potatoes*
éplucher	*to peel*

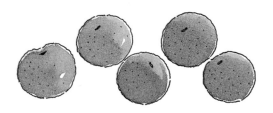

sing. **l'orange** (f)
orange

plural les oranges
oranges

sent-ence Je vois cinq **oranges**.
I see five oranges.

vocab.

cinq	*five*
orange	*orange*
le jus d'oranges	*orange juice*
le citron	*lemon*

sing. **la fraise**
strawberry

plural les fraises
strawberries

sent-ence Pierre mange six **fraises**.
Peter eats six strawberries.

vocab.

six	*six*
la confiture	*jam*
le sucre	*sugar*
manger	*to eat*

sing. **le radis**
radish

plural les radis
radishes

sentence Ces sept **radis** sont rouges.
These seven radishes are red.

vocab.

sept	*seven*
rouge	*red*
blanc	*white*
le légume	*vegetable*

sing. **la framboise**
raspberry

plural les framboises
raspberries

sent-ence Marc mange huit **framboises**.
Mark eats eight raspberries.

vocab.

huit	*eight*
rose	*pink*
le framboisier	*raspberry bush*
la glace	*ice-cream*

sing.

le chou de Bruxelles
Brussels sprout

plural

les choux de Bruxelles
Brussels sprouts

sent- ence

Je vois neuf **choux de Bruxelles**.
I see nine Brussels sprouts.

vocab.

neuf	*nine*
le jardin	*garden*
le marché	*market*
voir	*to see*

○ LES FRUITS ET LES LEGUMES

sing. **le fruit**
fruit

plural les fruits
fruits/pieces of fruit

sent- ence Je compte dix **fruits**.
I count ten pieces of fruit.

vocab.

dix	*ten*
l'ananas (m)	*pineapple*
le raisin	*grape*
la poire	*pear*

sing. **le chat**
cat

plural les chats
cats

**sent-
ence** Ce **chat** ronronne.
This cat is purring.

vocab.

la ferme	*farm*
le chaton	*kitten*
le panier	*basket*
miauler	*to miaow*

● LA FERME

sing. **le chien**
dog

plural les chiens
dogs

sent-ence Le **chien** a des taches brunes.
The dog has brown spots.

vocab.

la laisse	*lead*
le chiot	*puppy*
la niche	*kennel*
aboyer	*to bark*

sing. **la vache**
cow

plural les vaches
cows

sent-ence L'agriculteur trait la **vache**.
The farmer milks the cow.

vocab.

le lait	*milk*
le veau	*calf*
l'étable (f)	*cowshed*
meugler	*to moo*

sing. **le cheval**
horse

plural les chevaux
horses

sentence Le **cheval** mange de l'avoine.
The horse eats oats.

vocab.

l'avoine (f)	*oats*
le poulain	*foal*
la prairie	*meadow*
hennir	*to neigh*

sing. **l'oie** (f)
goose

plural les oies
geese

sentence Les **oies** cacardent.
The geese are honking.

vocab.

le canard	*duck*
le dindon	*turkey*
le paon	*peacock*
cacarder	*to honk*

sing. **le coq**
cockerel

plural les coqs
cockerels

sentence Le **coq** chante fort.
The cockerel crows loudly.

vocab.

la poule	*hen*
le poussin	*chick*
le poulailler	*henhouse*
chanter	*to crow*

sing.

le cochon
pig

plural

les cochons
pigs

**sent-
ence**

Le **cochon** grogne fort.
The pig grunts loudly.

vocab.

le lard	*bacon*
le porc	*pork*
la porcherie	*pigsty*
grogner	*to grunt*

sing. **le lapin**
rabbit

plural les lapins
rabbits

**sent-
ence** Le **lapin** mange de l'herbe.
The rabbit eats grass.

vocab.

l'herbe (f)	*grass*
le mouton	*sheep*
la chèvre	*goat*
l'âne (m)	*donkey*

sing. **le nichoir**
nesting-box

plural les nichoirs
nesting-boxes

sentence L'oiseau habite dans le **nichoir**.
The bird lives in the nesting box.

vocab.

le bois	*wood*
le nid	*nest*
l'œuf (m)	*egg*
la paille	*straw*

sing. **l'oiseau** (m)
bird

plural les oiseaux
birds

sent-ence L'**oiseau** chante un beau chant.
The bird sings a beautiful song.

vocab.

l'aile (f)	*wing*
le bec	*beak*
la plume	*feather*
voler	*to fly*

sing. **la pomme de pin**
pine cone

plural les pommes de pin
pine cones

sent-ence Je trouve une **pomme de pin**.
I find a pine cone.

vocab.

le pin	*pine tree*
le sapin	*fir tree*
le conifère	*conifer*
Noël	*Christmas*

sing.

la grenouille
frog

plural

les grenouilles
frogs

sent-ence

La **grenouille** saute haut.
The frog jumps high.

vocab.

le têtard	*tadpole*
l'étang (m)	*pond*
le ruisseau	*stream*
sauter	*to jump*

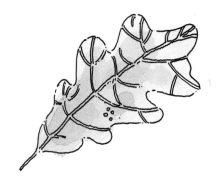

sing.

la feuille
leaf

plural

les feuilles
leaves

sentence

La **feuille** est verte.
The leaf is green.

vocab.

l'arbre (m)	*tree*
la branche	*branch*
le tronc	*trunk*
la fleur	*flower*

sing.

le lièvre
hare

plural

les lièvres
hares

**sent-
ence**

Le **lièvre** court dans le bois.
The hare runs through the wood.

vocab.

le pelage	*fur*
rapide/vite	*fast*
lent	*slow*
courir	*to run*

sing.

le marron
horse chestnut

plural

les marrons
horse chestnuts

**sent-
ence**

Le **marron** tombe par terre.
The horse chestnut falls to the ground.

vocab.

la châtaigne	*sweet chestnut*
la bogue	*husk*
le châtaignier	*chestnut tree*
l'automne (m)	*autumn*

sing.

le gland
acorn

plural

les glands
acorns

**sent-
ence**

L'écureuil aime les **glands**.
The squirrel likes acorns.

vocab.

l'écureuil (m)	*squirrel*
le chêne	*oak tree*
la noix	*nut*
la feuille de chêne	*oak leaf*

sing. **la promenade**
walk

plural les promenades
walks

sent-ence Olivier fait une **promenade**.
Oliver goes for a walk.

vocab.

le promeneur	*walker*
la canne	*walking stick*
le sentier	*path*
se promener	*to walk*

60

sing. **le champignon**
mushroom

plural les champignons
mushrooms

sent- ence Je vois trois **champignons**.
I see three mushrooms.

vocab.

le champignon vénéneux	*toadstool*
la terre	*soil*
la pierre	*stone*
cueillir	*to pick*

sing. **le gorille**
gorilla

plural les gorilles
gorillas

sent-ence Le **gorille** regarde les enfants.
The gorilla looks at the children.

vocab.

l'animal (m)	*animal*
la banane	*banana*
le jardin zoologique	*zoo*
le singe	*monkey*

sing. **l'éléphant** (m)
elephant

plural les éléphants
elephants

sentence L'**éléphant** a une longue trompe.
The elephant has a long trunk.

vocab.

la trompe	*trunk*
la défense	*tusk*
long	*long*
l'oreille (f)	*ear*

sing.	**le lion** *lion*
plural	les lions *lions*
sent-ence	Le **lion** rugit fort. *The lion roars loudly.*

vocab.		
	la lionne	*lioness*
	le lionceau	*lion cub*
	chasser	*to hunt*
	rugir	*to roar*

sing. **le crocodile**
crocodile

plural les crocodiles
crocodiles

sentence Le **crocodile** est dangereux.
The crocodile is dangerous.

vocab.

l'alligator (m)	*alligator*
les mâchoires	*jaws*
la rivière	*river*
dangereux	*dangerous*

sing.　**l'ours** (m)
bear

plural　les ours
bears

sent-ence　L'**ours** adore le miel.
The bear loves honey.

vocab.

le miel	*honey*
l'ourson (m)	*bear cub*
la griffe	*paw*
brun	*brown*

66

sing.

le kangourou
kangaroo

plural

les kangourous
kangaroos

sent-ence

Le **kangourou** saute loin.
The kangaroo jumps a long way.

vocab.

sauter	*to jump*
la poche ventrale	*pouch*
le désert	*desert*
la jambe	*leg*

67

sing.

la mer
the sea

plural

les mers
seas

sent- ence

Nous habitons au bord de la **mer**.
We live by the sea.

vocab.

le voilier	*sailing boat*
la jetée	*pier*
le poisson	*fish*
l'étoile de mer (f)	*starfish*

sing.

la plage
beach

plural

les plages
beaches

sent-ence

Il fait chaud sur la **plage**.
It is hot on the beach.

vocab.

le parasol	*sunshade*
le coquillage	*shell*
chaud	*hot*
froid	*cold*

sing. **le château de sable**
sandcastle

plural les châteaux de sable
sandcastles

sent-ence Je construis un **château de sable**.
I build a sandcastle.

vocab.

le sable	*sand*
la pelle	*spade*
le drapeau	*flag*
construire	*to build*

sing. **le ballon**
ball

plural les ballons
balls

sent-ence Pierre joue avec le **ballon**.
Peter is playing with the ball.

vocab.

le football	football
le pied	foot
le but	goal
jouer au football	to play football

71

sing. **la piscine**
swimming pool

plural les piscines
swimming pools

sentence Je joue dans la **piscine**.
I play in the swimming pool.

vocab.

le maillot de bain	*swimsuit*
la douche	*shower*
mouillé	*wet*
s'amuser	*to enjoy oneself*

○ LES VACANCES

sing. **la raquette**
racket

plural les raquettes
rackets

**sent-
ence** Je joue au tennis avec une **raquette**.
I play tennis with a racket.

vocab.

le joueur/la joueuse	*player*
le filet	*net*
le badminton	*badminton*
le tennis	*tennis*

sing.

la corde à sauter
skipping rope

plural

les cordes à sauter
skipping ropes

**sent-
ence**

Sophie a une nouvelle **corde à sauter**.
Sophy has a new skipping rope.

vocab.

la gymnastique	*gymnastics*
le/la gymnaste	*gymnast*
la culbute	*somersault*
sauter à la corde	*to skip*

74

sing. **le puzzle**
puzzle

plural les puzzles
puzzles

sent-ence Elle fait un **puzzle** difficile.
She does a difficult puzzle.

vocab.

difficile	*difficult*
facile	*easy*
le jeu	*game*
faire un puzzle	*to do a puzzle*

75

sing. **le nageur** (m)/**la nageuse** (f)
swimmer

plural les nageurs/les nageuses
swimmers

sent-ence Elle est une bonne **nageuse**.
She is a good swimmer.

vocab.

la natation	*swimming*
plonger	*to dive*
le tremplin	*springboard*
nager	*to swim*

sing.

le coureur/la coureuse
runner

plural

les coureurs/les coureuses
runners

sent-ence

Mon oncle est un bon **coureur**.
My uncle is a good runner.

vocab.

le sport	*sport*
la compétition	*competition*
sportif	*athletic*
courir	*to run*

77

sing. **le vent**
wind

plural les vents
winds

sentence J'entends le souffle du **vent**.
I hear the wind blowing.

vocab.

calme	*still/windless*
le pare-vent	*wind-break*
la girouette	*weather vane*
souffler	*to blow*

78

sing.

l'orage (m)
thunderstorm

plural

les orages
thunderstorms

sentence

Je n'aime pas les **orages**.
I don't like thunderstorms.

vocab.

violent	*violent*
le tonnerre	*thunder*
la foudre	*lightning*
le bruit	*noise*

sing.

le parapluie
umbrella

plural

les parapluies
umbrellas

sentence

Je m'abrite sous le **parapluie**.
I shelter under the umbrella.

vocab.

la pluie	*rain*
l'imperméable (m)	*raincoat*
la botte	*boot*
pleuvoir	*to rain*

sing. **le soleil**
sun

plural les soleils
suns

sentence Le **soleil** brille en été.
The sun shines in summer.

vocab.

l'été (m)	*summer*
le printemps	*spring*
le chapeau de soleil	*sun hat*
les lunettes de soleil	*sunglasses*

81

 sing. **la boule de neige**
snowball

 plural les boules de neige
snowballs

sent-ence Je fais deux **boules de neige**.
I make two snowballs.

vocab.

la neige	*snow*
le flocon	*snowflake*
l'hiver (m)	*winter*
le verglas	*black ice*

82

sing. | **la patinoire**
ice rink

plural | les patinoires
ice rinks

sentence | Nous patinons sur la **patinoire**.
We skate on the ice rink.

vocab.

le gel	*frost*
la glace	*ice*
le patin	*ice skate*
patiner	*to skate*

sing. **la bicyclette**
bicycle

plural les bicyclettes
bicycles

sent- ence J'ai une **bicyclette** orange.
I have an orange bicycle.

vocab.

le/la cycliste	*cyclist*
la selle	*saddle*
le pneu	*tyre*
la rue	*road*

○ LES MOYENS DE TRANSPORT

sing.   **la moto**
motorcycle

plural   les motos
motorcycles

sent-ence   Mon frère a une **moto**.
My brother has a motorcycle.

vocab.

le casque	*helmet*
la roue	*wheel*
le guidon	*handlebars*
le moteur	*engine*

85

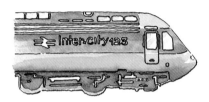

sing.

le train
train

plural

les trains
trains

sent-ence

Sarah voyage en **train**.
Sarah is travelling by train.

vocab.

la gare	*station*
le chemin de fer	*railway*
le wagon	*carriage*
le billet	*ticket*

sing. **l'autobus** (m)
bus

plural les autobus
buses

sent-ence Nous voyageons par **autobus**.
We travel by bus.

vocab.

l'arrêt d'autobus (m)	*bus stop*
la ligne d'autobus	*bus route*
aller	*to go*
voyager	*to travel*

87

sing. **le camion**
lorry

plural les camions
lorries

sent-ence Le **camion** transporte du sable.
The lorry carries sand.

vocab.

le conducteur	*driver*
le chargement	*load*
lourd	*heavy*
transporter	*to carry/transport*

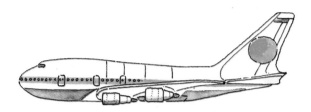

sing. **l'avion** (m)
aeroplane

plural les avions
aeroplanes

sentence Papa voyage en **avion**.
Dad travels by aeroplane.

vocab.

l'aéroport (m)	*airport*
le pilote	*pilot*
le départ	*departure*
l'arrivée (f)	*arrival*

sing.

la voiture
car

plural

les voitures
cars

sent-ence

Maman a une **voiture** bleue.
Mum has a blue car.

vocab.

le trafic	*traffic*
l'automobiliste (m/f)	*motorist*
l'autoroute (f)	*motorway*
conduire	*to drive*

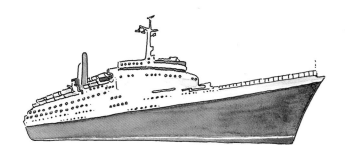

sing.

le bateau
boat

plural

les bateaux
boats

sent-ence

Le **bateau** navigue sur la mer.
The boat sails on the sea.

vocab.

le voyage en bateau	*boat trip*
le matelot	*sailor*
le capitaine	*captain*
naviguer	*to sail*

sing.

le peintre
painter

plural

les peintres
painters

sentence

Le **peintre** peint le mur.
The painter is painting the wall.

vocab.

la peinture	*paint*
le pinceau	*paintbrush*
le tableau	*painting*
peindre	*to paint*

sing. **le coiffeur**
hairdresser

plural les coiffeurs
hairdressers

sentence Le **coiffeur** coupe mes cheveux.
The hairdresser cuts my hair.

vocab.

les cheveux	*hair*
la coiffeur	*hair do*
les ciseaux	*scissors*
couper	*to cut*

93

sing. **le médecin**
doctor

plural les médecins
doctors

sentence Ce **médecin** m'a guéri.
This doctor has cured me.

vocab.

malade	*ill*
sain	*healthy*
le médicament	*medicine*
guérir	*to cure*

94

sing. **le boucher**
butcher

plural les bouchers
butchers

sentence Le **boucher** vend de la viande.
The butcher sells meat.

vocab.

la boucherie	*butcher's shop*
la saucisse	*sausage*
la viande	*meat*
vendre	*to sell*

sing. **le serveur**
waiter

plural les serveurs
waiters

sentence Le **serveur** sert une boisson.
The waiter is serving a drink.

vocab.

le café	*coffee*
le thé	*tea*
l'addition (f)	*bill*
servir	*to serve*

sing. **l'architecte** (m)
architect

plural les architectes
architects

sentence L'**architecte** dessine des plans.
The architect draws plans.

vocab.

le plan	plan
la table à dessin	drawing board
la maison	house
l'appartement (m)	flat

sing.

le boulanger
baker

plural

les boulangers
bakers

**sent-
ence**

Le **boulanger** cuit du pain.
The baker bakes bread.

vocab.

le pain	*bread*
le gâteau	*cake*
le four	*oven*
la boulangerie	*baker's shop*

sing. **l'agriculteur** (m)
farmer

plural les agriculteurs
farmers

sent-ence L'**agriculteur** est aux champs.
The farmer is in the field.

vocab.

le champ	*field*
le blé	*wheat*
le tracteur	*tractor*
la charrue	*plough*

sing. **le shampooing**
shampoo

plural les shampooings
shampoos

sent-ence Où est le **shampooing**?
Where is the shampoo?

vocab.

le sèche-cheveux	*hairdryer*
la tresse	*plait*
la bouteille	*bottle*
rincer	*to rinse*

sing.

la brosse à dents
toothbrush

plural

les brosses à dents
toothbrushes

sent-ence

Donne-moi ma **brosse à dents**.
Give me my toothbrush.

vocab.

le dentifrice	*toothpaste*
le gobelet	*beaker*
se brosser les dents	*to brush one's teeth*
la bouche	*mouth*

sing.

le bain
bath

plural

les bains
baths

sent-ence

Ils prennent un **bain** chaque jour.
They have a bath every day.

vocab.

la salle de bains	*bathroom*
le robinet	*tap*
la mousse	*foam*
le gant de toilette	*flannel*

102

sing. **la serviette**
towel

plural les serviettes
towels

sentence Je m'essuie avec une **serviette**.
I dry myself with a towel.

vocab.

humide	*damp*
sec	*dry*
le porte-serviettes	*towel rail*
s'essuyer	*to dry oneself*

sing. **le peigne**
comb

plural les peignes
combs

sent-ence Le **peigne** est dans l'armoire.
The comb is in the cupboard.

vocab.

la brosse	*hairbrush*
l'armoire (f)	*cupboard*
l'épingle à cheveux (f)	*hair-clip*
peigner	*to comb*

sing.

le pyjama
pyjamas

plural

les pyjamas
pyjamas

sent- ence

Tom met son **pyjama**.
Tom puts on his pyjamas.

vocab.

dormir	*to sleep*
se déshabiller	*to undress*
s'habiller	*to dress*
la pantoufle	*slipper*

sing. **la robe de chambre**
dressing gown

plural les robes de chambre
dressing gowns

sent-ence Elle porte une **robe de chambre**.
She is wearing a dressing gown.

vocab.

la chambre	*bedroom*
le soir	*evening*
la nuit	*night*
le jour	*day*

sing. **le rêve**
dream

plural les rêves
dreams

sent-ence J'ai fait un beau **rêve** cette nuit.
I had a nice dream last night.

vocab.

la lune	*moon*
l'étoile (f)	*star*
rêver	*to dream*
se réveiller	*to wake up*

107

sing.

le conte
story

plural

les contes
stories

sentence

Connais-tu un **conte** de fée?
Do you know a fairy story?

vocab.

raconter	*to tell*
le lit	*bed*
le livre d'images	*picture book*
regarder	*to look at*

INDEX

bathroom	la salle de bains, 102
beach	la plage, 69
beak	le bec, 53
beaker	le gobelet, 101
bear	l'ours (m), 66
bear cub	l'ourson (m), 66
bed	le lit, 108
bedroom	la chambre, 106
beneath	au-dessous, 17
bicycle	la bicyclette, 84
big	grand, 10
bill	l'addition (f), 96
bird	l'oiseau (m), 53
blackboard	le tableau, 24
black ice	le verglas, 82
blot	la tache, 31
(to) blow	souffler, 78
boat	le bateau, 91
boat trip	le voyage en bateau, 91
book	le livre, 30
boot	la botte, 80
boy	le garçon, 26
branch	la branche, 56
bread	le pain, 98
broom	le balai, 18
brother	le frère, 11
brown	brun, 66
(to) brush one's teeth	se brosser les dents, 101
Brussels sprout	le chou de Bruxelle, 42
bucket	le seau, 15
(to) build	construire, 70
bus	l'autobus (m), 87
bus route	la ligne d'autobus, 87

bus stop	l'arrêt d'autobus (m), 87
butcher	le boucher, 95
butcher's shop	la boucherie, 95
(to) buy	acheter, 36

C

cake	le gateau, 98
calf	le veau, 46
captain	le capitaine, 91
car	la voiture, 90
carpet	le tapis, 14
carriage	le wagon, 86
cat	le chat, 44
ceiling	le plafond, 17
chalk	la craie, 24
chestnut tree	le châtaignier, 58
chick	le poussin, 49
child	l'enfant (m/f), 11
Christmas	Noël, 54
classroom	la classe, 25
(to) clean	nettoyer, 14
clean/neat	propre, 16
(to) climb	grimper, 17
cockerel	le coq, 49
coffee	le café, 96
cold	froid, 69
(to) comb	peigner, 104
comb	le peigne, 104
competition	la compétition, 77
conifer	le conifère, 54
(to) cook	cuisiner, 20
cook	le cuisinier, 21
cooker	la cuisinière, 20

cousin (male)	le cousin, 12
cousin (female)	la cousine, 12
cow	la vache, 46
cowshed	l'étable (f), 46
crocodile	le crocodile, 65
(to) crow	chanter, 49
(to) cry	pleurer, 13
cupboard	l'armoire (f), 104
(to) cure	guérir, 94
(to) cut	couper, 93
cutlery	le couvert, 23
cyclist	le/la cycliste, 84

D

damp	humide, 103
dangerous	dangereux, 65
daughter	la fille, 10
day	le jour, 106
departure	le départ, 89
desert	le désert, 67
dictionary	le dictionnaire, 30
difficult	difficile, 75
dirty	sale, 16
(to) dive	plonger, 76
doctor	le médecin, 94
dog	le chien, 45
donkey	l'âne (m), 51
(to) draw	dessiner, tracer, 32
drawing board	la table de dessin, 97
(to) dream	rêver, 107
dream	rêve, 107
(to) dress	s'habiller, 105
dressing gown	la robe de chambre, 106

(to) drink	boire, 22
(to) drive	conduire, 90
driver	le conducteur, 88
dry	sec, 103
(to) dry oneself	s'essuyer, 103
duck	le canard, 48
dust	la poussière, 14
dustbin	la poubelle, 18
dustpan	la pelle à poussière, 18

E

ear	l'oreille (f), 63
easy	facile, 75
(to) eat	manger, 39
egg	l'œuf (m), 52
eight	huit, 41
elephant	l'éléphant (m), 63
empty	vide, 15
engine	le moteur, 85
English	l'anglais (m), 26
(to) enjoy oneself	s'amuser, 72
evening	le soir, 106
exercise	l'exercice (m), 28
exercise book	le cahier, 28

F

family	la famille, 8
farm	la ferme, 44
farmer	l'agriculteur (m), 99
fast	rapide/vite, 57
father	le père, 9
feather	la plume, 53
field	le champ, 99

figure	le chiffre, 32
(to) fill	remplir, 15
fir tree	le sapin, 54
fish	le poisson, 68
five	cinq, 38
flag	le drapeau, 70
flannel	le gant de toilette, 102
flat	l'appartement (m), 97
floor	le sol, 18
flower	la fleur, 56
(to) fly	voler, 53
foal	le poulain, 47
foam	la mousse, 102
foot	le pied, 71
football	le football, 71
fork	la fourchette, 23
four	quatre, 31
French	le français, 26
friend	l'ami (m)/l'amie (f), 27
friendly	gentil/amical, 27
frog	la grenouille, 55
frost	le gel, 83
fruit	le fruit, 43
(to) fry	frire, 21
frying pan	la poêle, 21
full	plein, 15
fur	le pelage, 57

G

game	le jeu, 75
garden	le jardin, 42
girl	la fille, 25
glass	le verre, 22

114

(to) go	aller, 87
goal	le but, 71
goat	la chèvre, 51
goose	l'oie (f), 48
gorilla	le gorille, 62
grandfather	le grand-père, 9
grandmother	la grand-mère, 8
grape	le raisin, 43
grass	l'herbe (f), 51
green	vert, 34
(to) grunt	grogner, 50
gymnast	le/la gymnast, 74
gymnastics	la gymnastique, 74

H

hair	les cheveux, 93
hairbrush	la brosse, 104
hair-clip	l'épingle à cheveux (f), 104
hair do	la coiffure, 93
hairdresser	le coiffeur, 93
hair-dryer	le sèche-cheveux, 100
handlebars	le guidon, 85
hare	le lièvre, 57
healthy	sain, 94
heavy	lourd, 88
helmet	le casque, 85
hen	la poule, 49
henhouse	le poulailler, 49
homework	le devoir, 26
honey	le miel, 66
(to) honk	cacarder, 48
horse	le cheval, 47
horse chestnut	le marron, 58

house	la maison, 77
housework	le ménage, 14
(to) hunt	chasser, 64
husband	l'époux (m), 9
husk	la bogue, 58

I

ice	la glace, 83
ice-cream	la glace, 41
ice rink	la patinoire, 83
ice skate	le patin, 83
ill	malade, 94
ink	l'encre (f), 31

J

jam	la confiture, 39
jaws	les mâchoires, 65
juice	le jus, 35
(to) jump	sauter, 67

K

kangaroo	le kangourou, 67
kennel	la niche, 45
kitchen	la cuisine, 20
kitten	le chaton, 44
kiwi fruit	le kiwi, 35
knife	le couteau, 23

L

ladder	l'échelle (f), 17
lead	la laisse, 45
leaf	la feuille, 56
leg	la jambe, 67

lemon	le citron, 38
lesson	la leçon, 25
letter	la lettre, 31
lightning	la foudre, 79
(to) like/love	aimer, 27
line	la ligne, 32
lion	le lion, 64
lion cub	le lionceau, 64
lioness	la lionne, 64
long	long, 63
(to) look at	regarder, 108
lorry	le camion, 88

M

man	l'homme (m), 9
market	le marché, 42
mashed potatoes	la purée, 37
mathematics	le calcul, 26
meadow	la prairie, 47
(to) measure	mesurer, 32
meat	la viande, 95
medicine	le médicament, 94
melon	le melon, 34
(to) miaow	miauler, 44
milk	le lait, 46
mistake	l'erreur (f), 28
monkey	le singe, 62
(to) moo	meugler, 46
moon	la lune, 107
mother	la mère, 8
motorcycle	la moto, 85
motorist	l'automobiliste (m/f), 90
motorway	l'autoroute (f), 90

mouth	la bouche, 101
mushroom	le champignon, 61
music	la musique, 33

N

(to) neigh	hennir, 47
nest	le nid, 52
nesting box	le nichoir, 52
net	le filet, 73
niece	la nièce, 13
night	la nuit, 106
nine	neuf, 42
noise	le bruit, 79
note	la note, 33
nut	la noix, 59

O

oak	la chêne, 59
oak leaf	la feuille de chêne, 59
oats	l'avoine (f), 47
oil	l'huile (f), 21
one	un/une, 34
orange	l'orange (f), 38
orange juice	le jus d'orange, 38
oven	le four, 98

P

page	la page, 30
(to) paint	peindre, 92
paint	la peinture, 92
paintbrush	le pinceau, 92
painter	le peintre, 92
painting	le tableau, 92

pancake	la crêpe, 21
parents	les parents, 9
path	le sentier, 60
paw	la griffe, 66
peacock	le paon, 48
pear	la poire, 43
(to) peel	éplucher, 37
peel	la pelure, 37
pencil	le crayon, 29
pencil case	le plumier, 29
pencil sharpener	le taille-crayon, 29
(to) pick	cueillir, 61
picture book	le livre d'images, 108
pier	la jetée, 68
pig	le cochon, 50
pigsty	la porcherie, 50
pilot	le pilote, 89
pineapple	l'ananas (m), 43
pine cone	la pomme de pin, 54
pine tree	le pin, 54
pink	rose, 41
pip	le pépin, 34
plait	la tresse, 100
plan	le plan, 97
plate	l'assiette (f), 22
(to) play	jouer, 13
(to) play football	jouer au football, 71
player	le joueur/la joueuse, 73
plough	la charrue, 99
pork	le porc, 50
potato	la pomme de terre, 37
pouch	la poche ventrale, 67
pupil	l'élève (m/f), 25

puzzle	le puzzle, 45
pyjamas	le pyjama, 105

R

rabbit	le lapin, 51
racket	la raquette, 73
radish	le radis, 40
railway	le chemin de fer, 86
(to) rain	pleuvoir, 80
rain	la pluie, 80
raincoat	l'imperméable (m), 80
raspberry	la framboise, 41
raspberry bush	le framboisier, 41
(to) read	lire, 30
red	rouge, 40
(to) rinse	rincer, 100
road	la rue, 84
(to) roar	rugir, 64
river	la rivière, 65
rubber	la gomme, 29
ruler	la règle, 32
(to) run	courir, 57, 77
runner	le coureur, 77

S

saddle	la selle, 84
(to) sail	naviguer, 91
sailing boat	le voilier, 68
sailor	le matelot, 91
sand	le sable, 70
sandcastle	le château de sable, 70
saucepan	la marmite, 20
saucer	la soucoupe, 22

sausage	la saucisse, 95
school	l'école (f), 24
schoolbag	le cartable, 29
scissors	les ciseaux, 93
sea	la mer, 68
(to) see	voir, 42
(to) sell	vendre, 95
sentence	la phrase, 28
(to) serve	servir, 96
seven	sept, 40
shampoo	le shampooing, 100
sheep	le mouton, 51
shell	le coquillage, 69
(to) shout	crier, 13
shower	la douche, 72
(to) sing	chanter, 33
sister	la soeur, 10
six	six, 39
(to) skate	patiner, 83
(to) skip	sauter à la corde, 74
skipping rope	la corde à sauter, 74
(to) sleep	dormir, 105
slipper	la pantoufle, 105
slow	lent, 57
small/little	petit, 10
(to) smile	sourire, 27
snow	la neige, 82
snowball	la boule de neige, 82
snowflake	le flocon, 82
soap	le savon, 19
soap dish	le porte-savon, 19
soil	la terre, 61
somersault	la culbute, 74

son	le fils, 11
song	la chanson, 33
sour	aigre, 35
spade	la pelle, 70
sponge	l'éponge (f), 16
spoon	la cuiller, 23
sport	le sport, 77
spring	le printemps, 81
springboard	le tremplin, 76
squirrel	l'écureuil (m), 59
stalk	le queue, 34
star	l'étoile (f), 107
starfish	l'étoile de mer (f), 68
station	la gare, 86
still/calm	calme, 78
(to) stir	remuer, 20
stone	la pierre, 61
story	le conte, 108
straw	la paille, 52
strawberry	la fraise, 39
stream	le ruisseau, 55
(to) study	étudier, 25
sugar	le sucre, 39
summer	l'été (m), 81
sun	le soleil, 81
sunglasses	les lunettes de soleil, 81
sun hat	le chapeau de soleil, 81
sunshade	le parasol, 69
(to) sweep	balayer, 18
sweet	doux, 35
sweet chestnut	la châtaigne, 58
(to) swim	nager, 76
swimmer	le nageur/la nageuse, 76

swimming	la natation, 76
swimming pool	la piscine, 72
swimsuit	le maillot de bain, 72

T

table	la table, 23
tap	le robinet, 102
tea	le thé, 96
teacher	l'institutrice (f)/l'instituteur (m), 24
(to) tell	raconter, 108
ten	dix, 43
tennis	le tennis, 73
three	trois, 36
thunder	le tonnerre, 79
thunderstorm	l'orage (m), 79
ticket	le billet, 86
title	le titre, 30
toadstool	le champignon vénéneux, 61
toddler	le petit enfant, 11
toothbrush	la brosse à dents, 101
toothpaste	le dentifrice, 101
towel	la serviette, 103
towel rail	le porte-serviette, 103
tractor	le tracteur, 99
traffic	le trafic, 90
train	le train, 86
(to) transport	transporter, 88
(to) travel	voyager, 87
tree	l'arbre (m), 56
trunk (elephant)	la trompe, 63
turkey	le dindon, 48
tusk	la défense, 63
two	deux, 35

tyre	le pneu, 84

U

umbrella	le parapluie, 80
uncle	l'oncle (m), 12
(to) undress	se déshabiller, 105

V

vacuum cleaner	l'aspirateur (m), 14
vegetable	le légume, 40
violent	violent, 79
(to) visit	visiter/rendre visite à, 12

W

waiter	le serveur, 96
(to) wake up	se réveiller, 107
(to) walk	se promener, 60
walk	la promenade, 60
walker	le promeneur, 60
walking stick	la canne, 60
warm/hot	chaud, 69
(to) wash	laver, 16
(to) wash oneself	se laver, 19
washbasin	le lavabo, 19
water	l'eau (f), 15
weather vane	la girouette, 78
wheat	le blé, 99
wheel	la roue, 85
(to) whistle	siffler, 33
white	blanc, 40
wife	l'épouse (f), 8
wind	le vent, 78
windbreak	le pare-vent, 78

window	la fenêtre, 16
wing	l'aile (f), 53
winter	l'hiver (m), 82
woman	la femme, 8
wood	le bois, 52
word	le mot, 28
(to) write	écrire, 24

Z

zoo	le jardin zoologique, 62